You Don't Know Jack!

Jessica M. Morrow

Copyright © 2014 Jessica M. Morrow

All rights reserved.

ISBN-13: 978-0615981338

DEDICATION

I wish to dedicate this book to my family & friends:
Daddy-doo & Mutti, Donna & Jim,
Lisa, Taylor, Darylee, Josh & Selah
Holly & Dylan
Mark, Dunja, Michael & Megan
Scott, Kathy, Nicky, Alex & Olivia
I wish to thank James for his many years of support, friendship, his typing skills and all his hard work.
I wish to thank Pamster for her friendship and for making me laugh and Patsy for her love, support and daily chats.
I love you All!

ACKNOWLEDGMENTS

I wish to thank all the rescuers, volunteers and owners for all your love, time, support, dedication and charity to save these amazing animals because they all deserve a chance.

You are ALL Guardian Angels.

You Don't Know Jack!

He can be lazy

He can be kind of crazy

And he can talk a lot of smack.

The reason I can say this is

because you don't know Jack.

He can be hairy

And he can look kind of scary

Even from the front or the back.

The reason I can say this is

because you don't know Jack.

His face is kind of scruffy

And he likes a bed that's fluffy

And he would never sleep in a shack.

The reason I can say this is

because you don't know Jack.

He has a strange growl

And sometimes he may howl

But he will never attack.

The reason I can say this is

because you don't know Jack.

He can be dirty

But most times he's clean.

So, just give him a little slack.

The reason I can say this is

because you don't know Jack.

He won't wear a hat that's puffy

And his clothes are rough and toughie

And these are just the facts.

The reason I can say this is

because you don't know Jack.

He has a friend named GiGi

The two are as happy as can be

And they've got each other's back

The reason I can say this is

GiGi is the best friend of Jack.

He'll play with his toy squirrel

And jump around and twirl

And he'll even do it for a snack.

The reason I can say this is

because you don't know Jack.

He'll chase a cat or a mouse

He'll even guard your house.

He'll always be a part of your pack.

The reason I can say this is

because you don't know Jack.

He won't be negative

And he'll always be positive.

He'll greet you at the door when you get back.

The reason I can say this is

because now you know Jack.

ABOUT THE AUTHOR

Jessica M. Morrow has been an artist since she was a little girl. Her talents have included painting, floral design, fashion design and a myriad of other mediums. She has been writing poetry all her life. She is also a Blu~e™ spiritual healer and Oneness™ Deeksha blessing giver. She has been involved with rescuing and humane animal causes and charities for over 20 years. She lives with two rescued mini-poodles; their affection inspired her to write this book.

www.ingramcontent.com/pod-product-compliance
Lightning Source LLC
Chambersburg PA
CBHW042218050426
42453CB00001BA/11